A MAP IS A PICTURE

A MAP

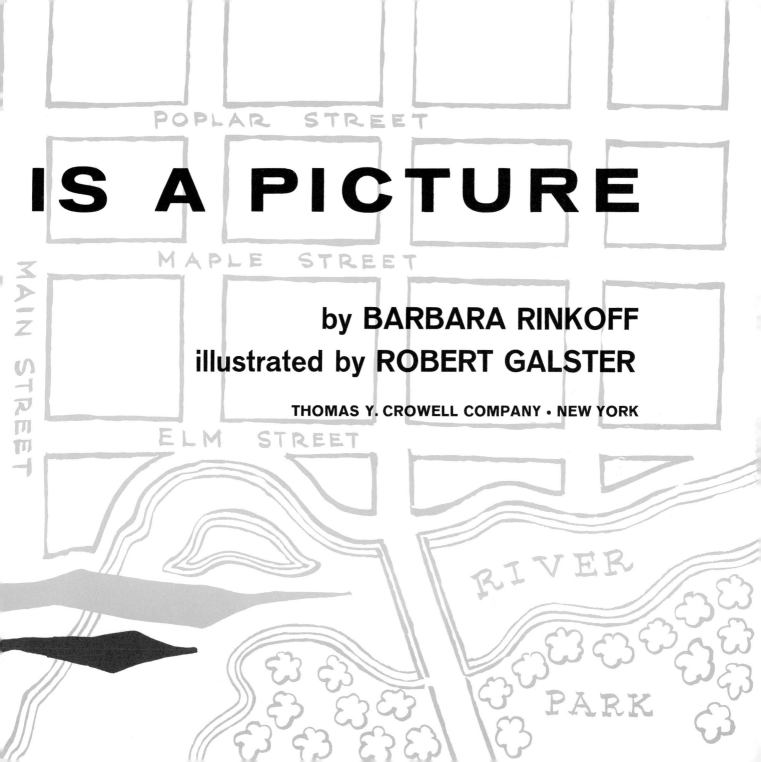

IS A PICTURE

by **BARBARA RINKOFF**
illustrated by **ROBERT GALSTER**

THOMAS Y. CROWELL COMPANY · NEW YORK

POPLAR STREET

MAPLE STREET

MAIN STREET

ELM STREET

RIVER

PARK

LET'S-READ-AND-FIND-OUT BOOKS

Special Adviser: *DR. ROMA GANS*, Professor Emeritus of Childhood Education, Teachers College, Columbia University.
Editor: *DR. FRANKLYN M. BRANLEY*, Coordinator of Educational Services, American Museum — Hayden Planetarium, consultant on science in elementary education.

The publisher is indebted to Frances Sullivan of the Wichita Public Library for help in preparing this book. The map of Wichita on page 27 is copyright © 1962 by Dietzgen/Kansas Blue Print. The map of Kansas on pages 28-29 is copyright by the American Automobile Association. Both are reproduced by kind permission. Copyright © 1965 by Barbara Rinkoff. Illustrations copyright © 1965 by Robert Galster. All rights reserved. No part of this book may be reproduced in any form, except by a reviewer, without the permission of the publisher. Manufactured in the United States of America. Library of Congress Catalog Card No. 65-11648.   1 2 3 4 5 6 7 8 9 10

A MAP IS A PICTURE

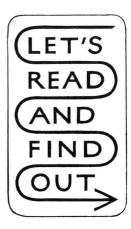

LET'S READ AND FIND OUT

Here is a treasure map. Long ago pirates made maps
like this one. They made a map to show where
they had buried their treasure of gold and jewels.
The directions on this treasure map are easy to follow. You can read them yourself.

TREASURE MAP

FROM HARBOR FOLLOW PATH
UP DEAD MAN HILL. TURN LEFT AT
BIG ROCK. WALK STRAIGHT 20 PACES.
TURN RIGHT AT FORK IN PATH.
WALK 10 PACES TO OAK TREE ON LEFT
SIDE OF PATH. DIG 4 FEET DOWN
ON SIDE OF OAK TREE THAT
HAS J. R. CARVED ON IT.

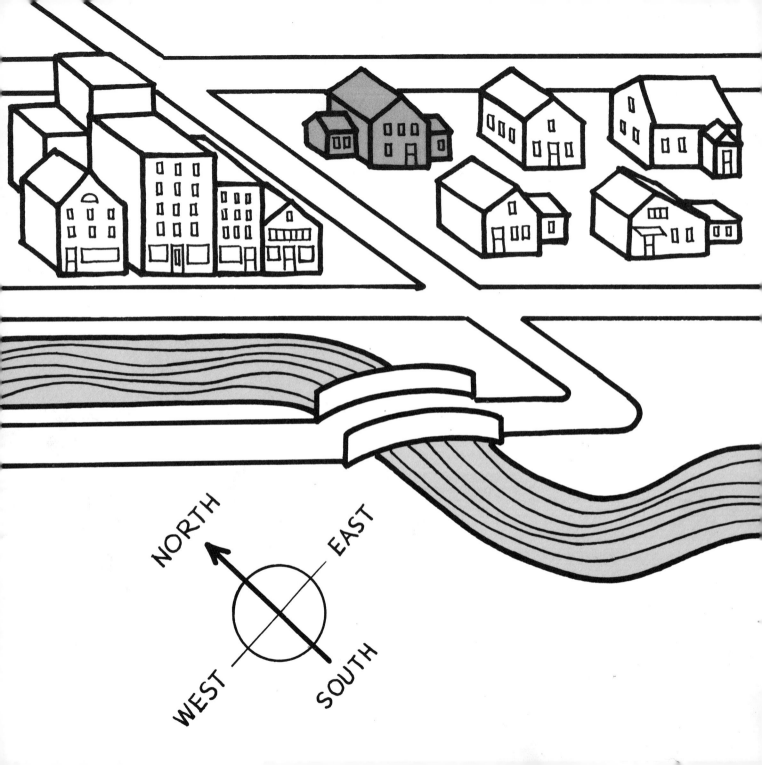

NORTH

EAST

WEST

SOUTH

Here is another kind of map. It is the map of a town. The arrow shows which way is north.
The front of the gray house faces north. You can tell because it faces in the same direction as the arrow points.

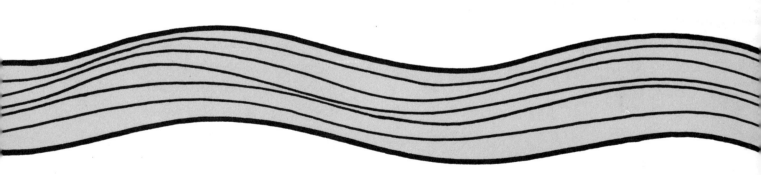

The opposite of north is south. The bridge is south of the house. The river under the bridge flows from east to west.

Here is a map of a larger town. This map has a KEY. These are some of the things the key tells you:

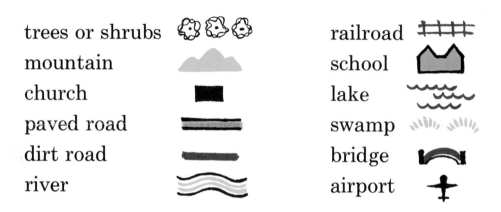

trees or shrubs		railroad	
mountain		school	
church		lake	
paved road		swamp	
dirt road		bridge	
river		airport	

Find the school and the railroad tracks. Find the airport, the lake, the river, the bridges, and the swamp.

On a map things are made smaller than they really are. If they were their real size they would not fit on the paper. One inch on this map would be a mile on the land. We say that the SCALE is one inch to one mile.

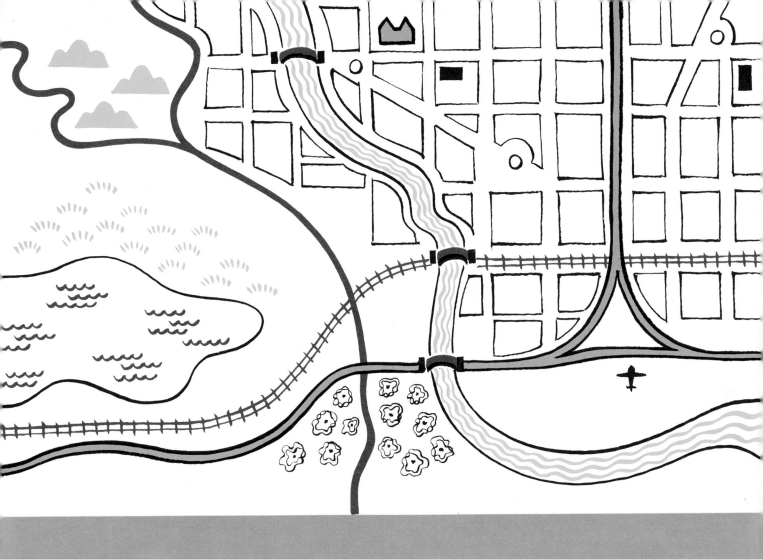

Measure the inches from the school to the airport.
Then you can change the inches to miles. That is
how far it really is from the school to the airport.

Each map has a different scale. One inch might stand for 10 miles or 20 miles, even hundreds of miles. In a map of outer space one inch may stand for millions of miles.

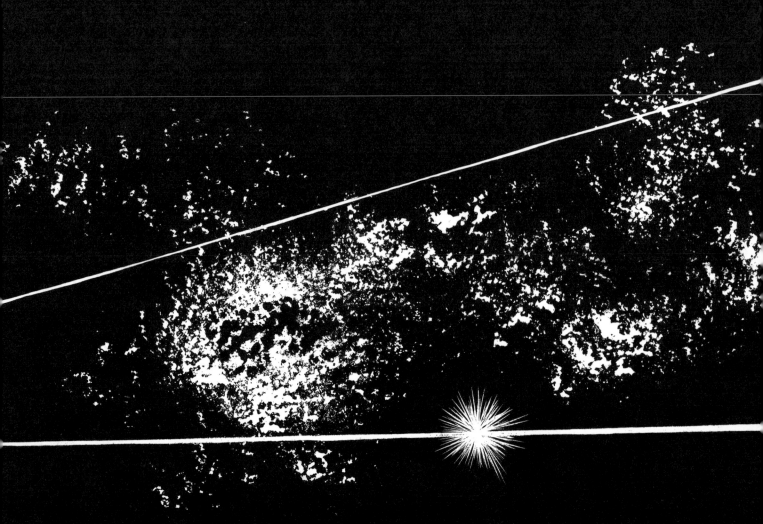

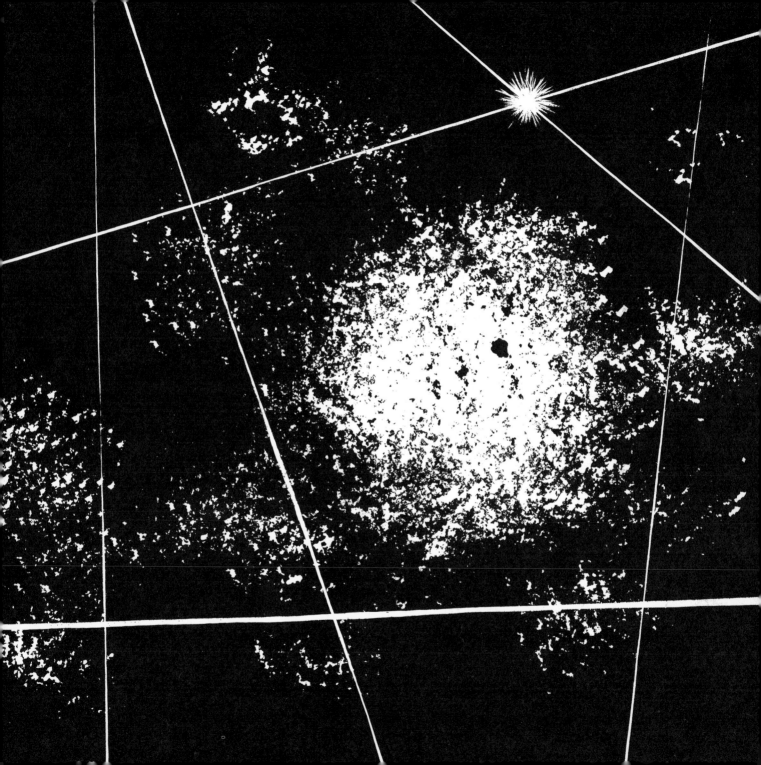

You can draw a map of your neighborhood. Use a key to show your house, your school, your favorite store. Maybe you can add the firehouse, the police station, the hospital, and the park. If you are near rivers or mountains or lakes you can put them on your map.

MAIN STREET

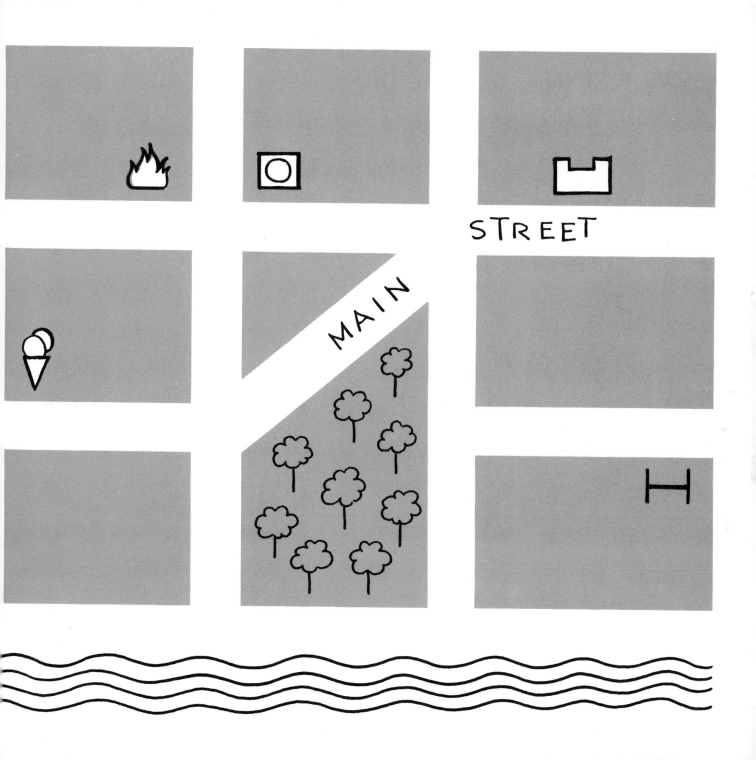

STREET

MAIN

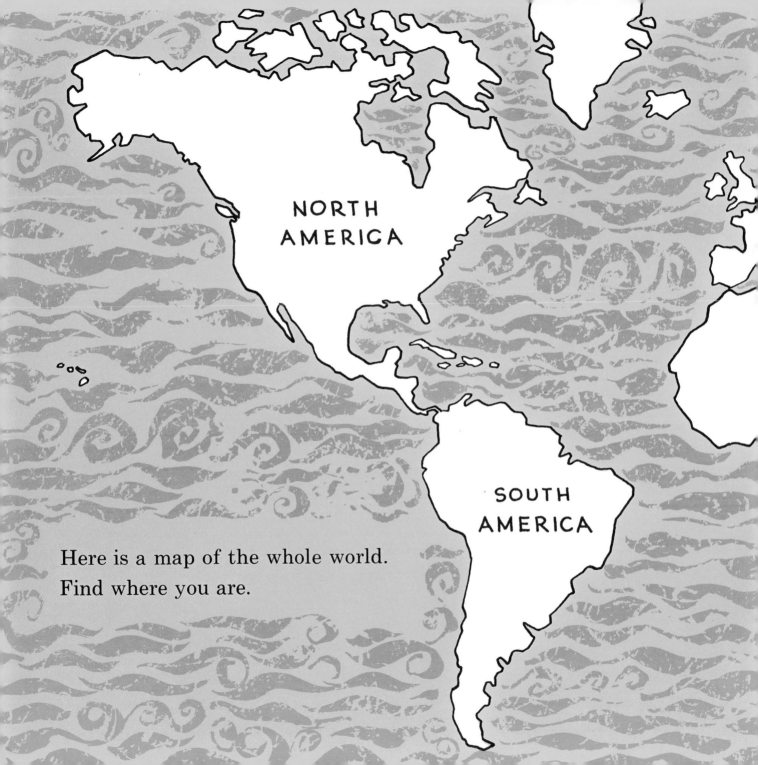

NORTH
AMERICA

SOUTH
AMERICA

Here is a map of the whole world.
Find where you are.

This is a map of a part of the world. It is the continent of North America. Find the United States.

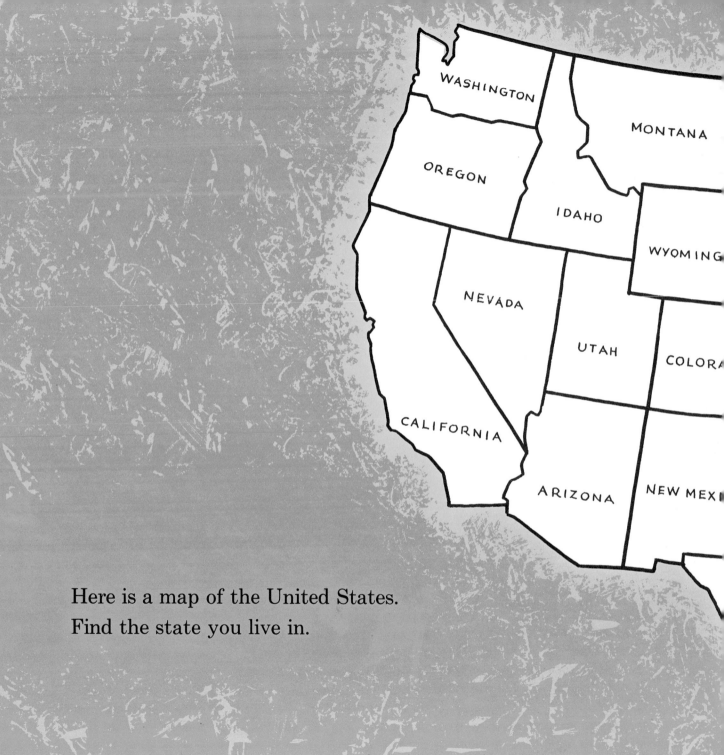

Here is a map of the United States.
Find the state you live in.

NORTON

OBERLIN

GOODLAND

COLBY

NORTH FORK SOLOMON RIVER

SOUTH FORK SOLOMON RIVER

SHARON SPRINGS

SMOKY HILL RIVER

SCOTT CITY

WALNUT CREEK

GARDEN CITY

DODGE CITY

ARKANSAS RIVER

Here is a map of the state of Kansas.
Find the city of Wichita.

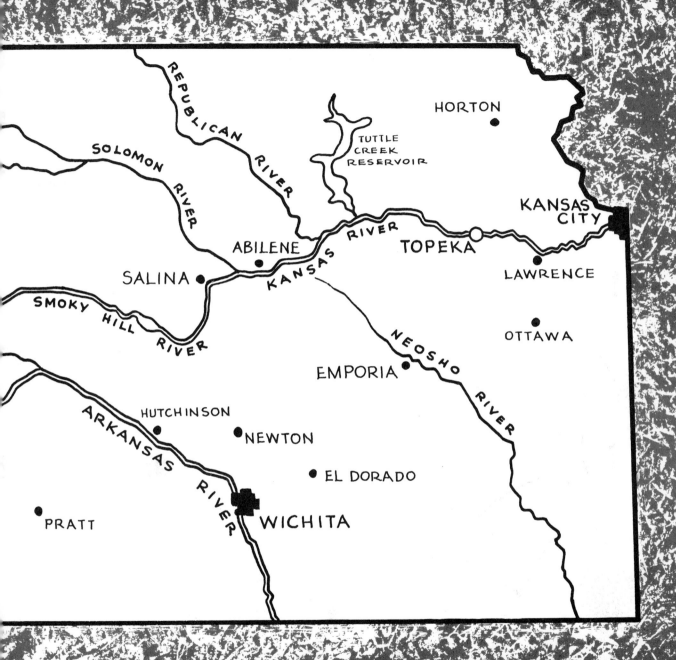

This is a map of part of Wichita. Find Estelle Street. On a map of your city you can find the street you live on.

There are maps of the world, continents, countries, states, cities, villages, towns, and neighborhoods. There are many other kinds of maps.

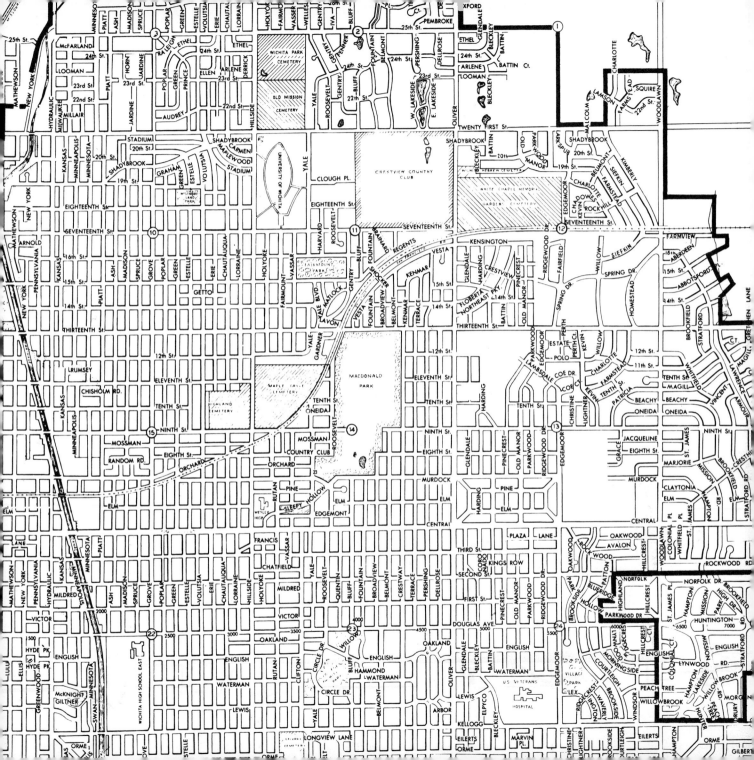

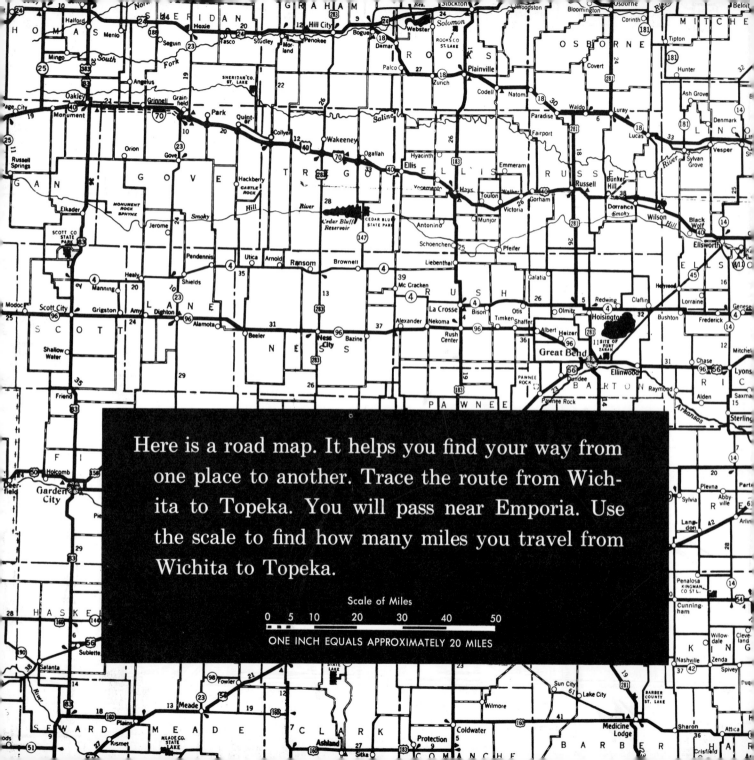

Here is a road map. It helps you find your way from one place to another. Trace the route from Wichita to Topeka. You will pass near Emporia. Use the scale to find how many miles you travel from Wichita to Topeka.

Scale of Miles

0   5 10   20   30   40   50

ONE INCH EQUALS APPROXIMATELY 20 MILES

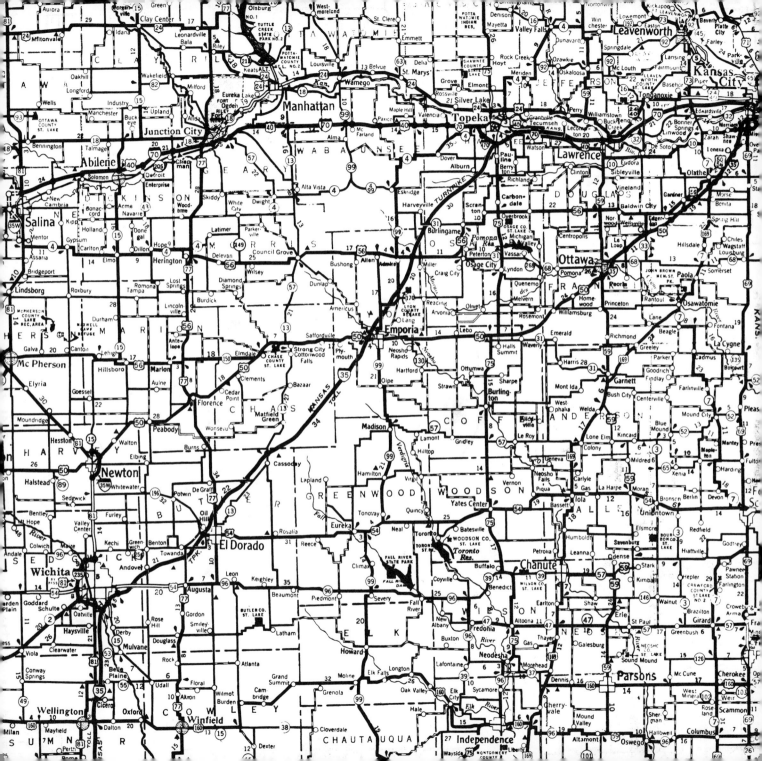

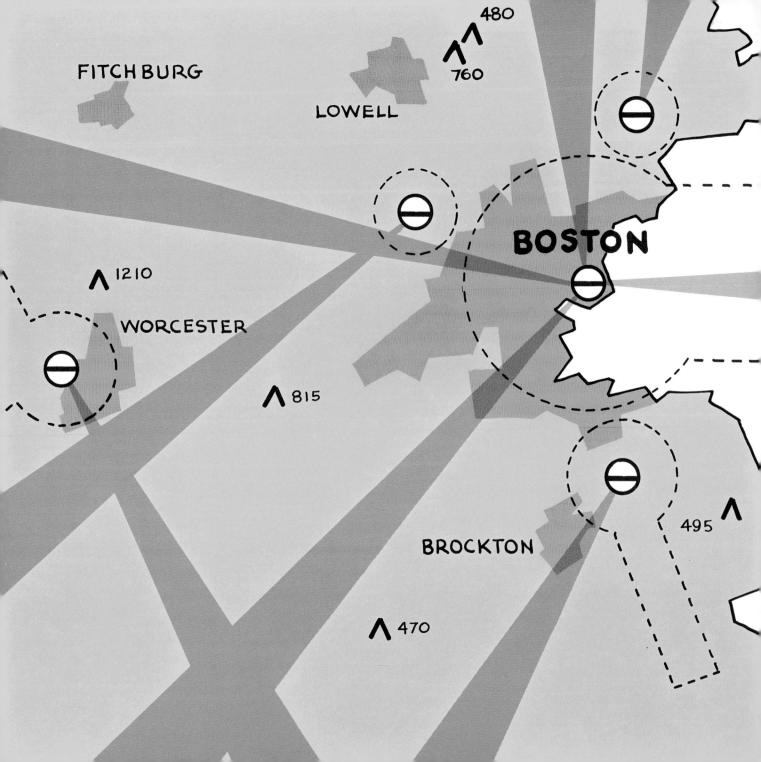

MASSACHUSETTS BAY

Here is an airway map. You can see the routes that airplanes fly. The pilot of the plane follows these paths in the sky just as you follow the roads on the ground to get from one place to another.

LANDING FIELDS

OBSTRUCTIONS   1200 FEET

RADIO RANGE

CONTROL AREAS

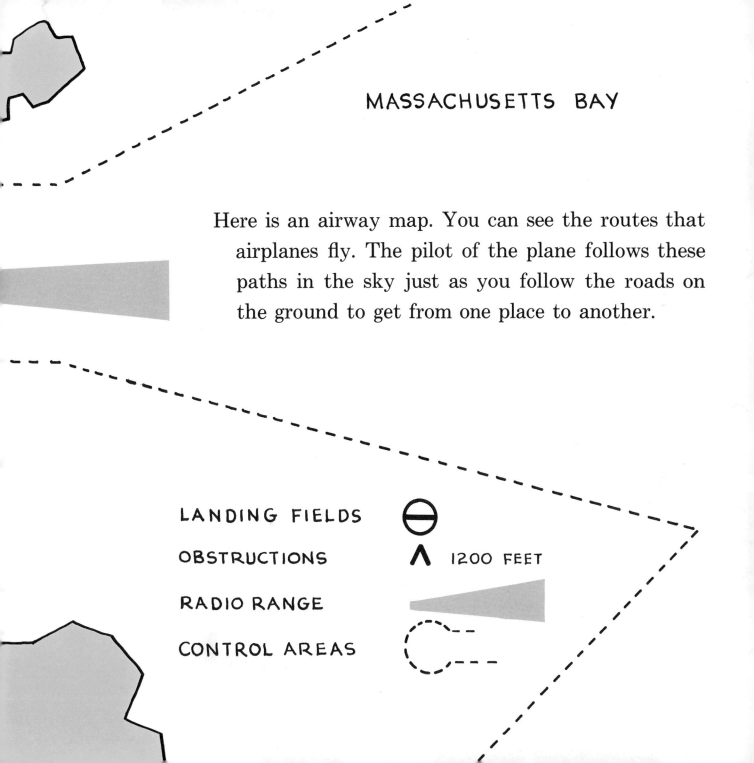

Your city has a map of its water pipes. If a pipe breaks, the repairman looks at the map. He sees where he must dig up the street to find the pipe.

On the next page is an agricultural map. You can look at the key to find where corn is grown, where cotton is produced, where trees and forests grow, and where peanuts are planted.

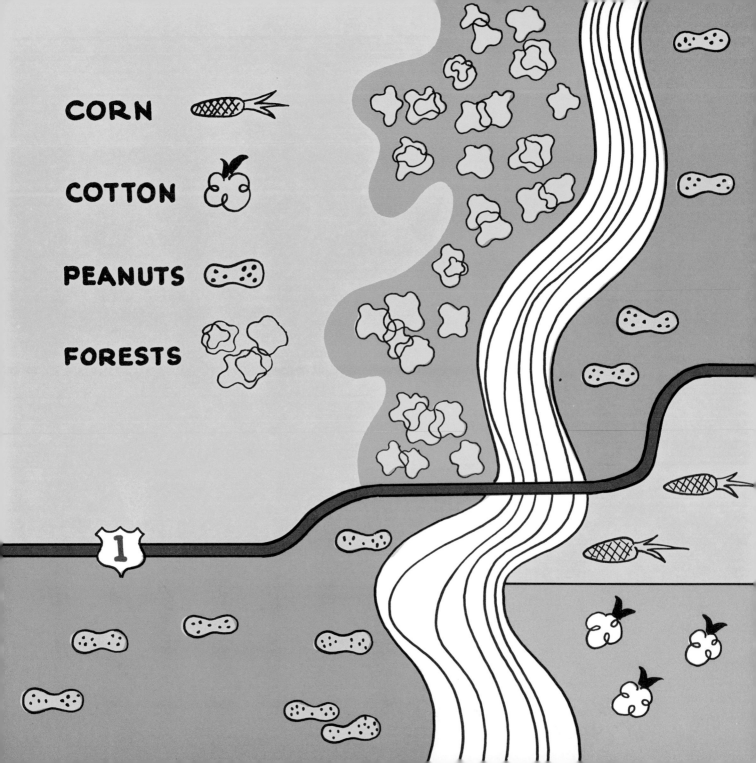

CORN

COTTON

PEANUTS

FORESTS

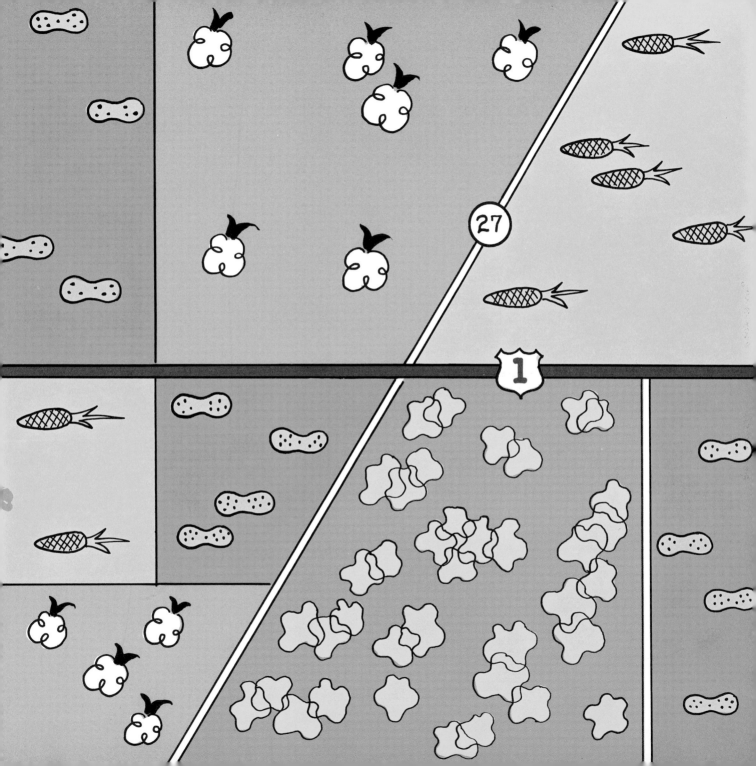

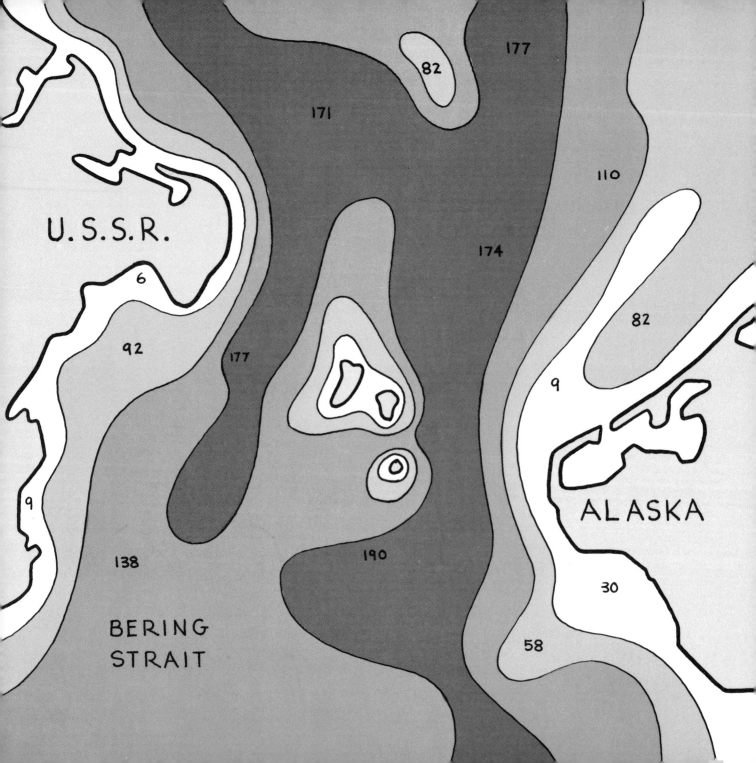

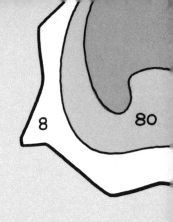

83

23

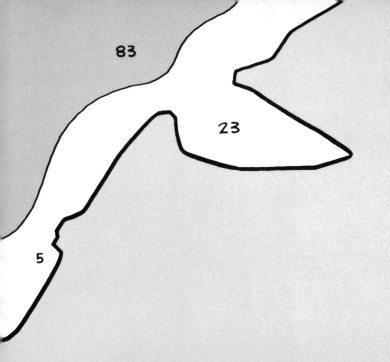

8   80

5

ALASKA

Here is a map of the sea. The map shows how deep
the water is. It shows where there are mountains
and valleys under the water.
A diver reads maps of the sea.

OCEAN DEPTH SHOWN IN FEET

12

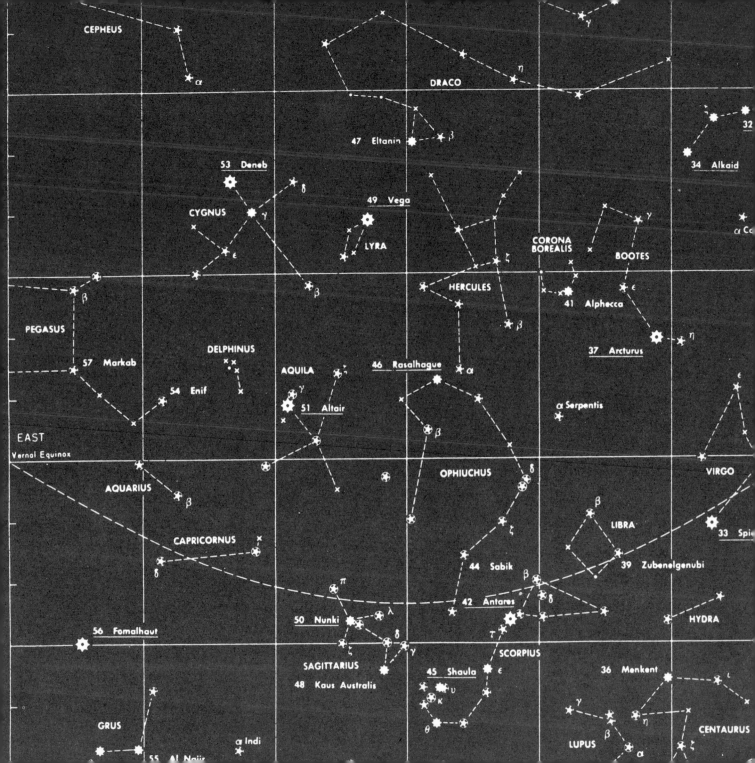

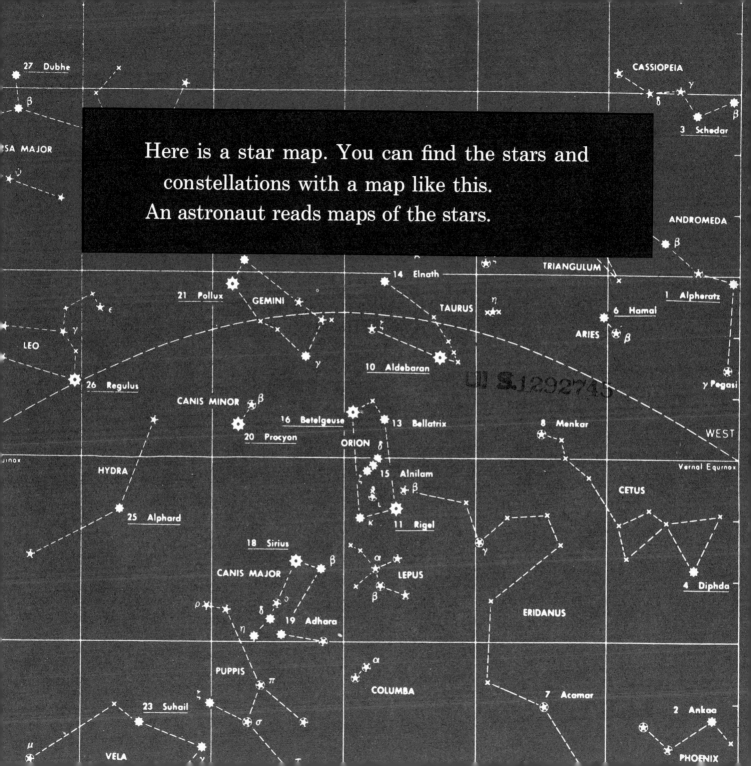

Here is a star map. You can find the stars and
constellations with a map like this.
An astronaut reads maps of the stars.

Get a road map of your state at a gas station. Find where you are. Trace the route you will take on your next trip.

Now *you* are reading a map.